Bakery

by Melissa Wagner
illustrated by Felipe Galindo

HOUGHTON MIFFLIN HARCOURT
School Publishers

Printed in China

ISBN-13: 978-0-547-02844-6
ISBN-10: 0-547-02844-X

5 6 7 8 0940 18 17 16 15 14 13 12
4500358727

On Saturday, I went to work with my family.
We left early in the morning.
It was still dark!

Dad opened the door.
I turned on the lights.
Lots of work had to be done
before we could open our
bakery.

In the kitchen, Dad made bread.
He added yeast, so the bread
was soft and light.
Grandma and Mom made cakes
and pies.
My job was to pour in nuts.

Dad put everything
into the hot oven.
Then Mom took the food
out of the oven.
When everything was cool, we
carried the food into the store.

Soon people came to the bakery.
Some people sat down to eat.
Some people took food home.
"I'd like a loaf of bread,"
Mr. Fox said.
I helped Grandma wrap the
bread in paper.

We sold all the bread and cookies, so Mom and Dad baked more in the kitchen.

I like the butter cookies best, so Mom gave me a few. Yum!

"They were great!" I told her.

At the end of the day, Dad and Grandma cleaned the kitchen. Mom and I cleaned the store.

Then we went home for dinner.
My family sat down at the table.
We talked about our day and
laughed at Dad's jokes.

We were very tired, so we went to bed early.
It was a busy day at our bakery!

Responding

What are three things that need to be done in the bakery? What does this tell you about work in a bakery? Make a chart.

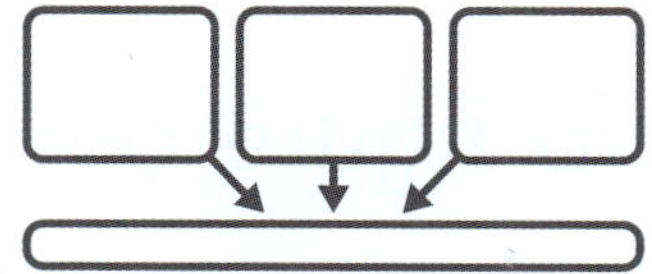

Talk About It

Text to Text Think of another story about people doing work. How is the work in this story different?

WORDS TO KNOW

done	**soon**
great	**talks**
laughs	**were**
paper	**work**

TARGET SKILL **Conclusions**

Use details to figure out more about the text.

TARGET STRATEGY **Monitor/Clarify**

Find ways to figure out what doesn't make sense.

GENRE **Realistic fiction** is a story that could happen in real life.